ESSENTIAL MANAGERS

W9-AMT-577

The Digital Revolution

ALAN CHARLESWORTH

London, New York, Munich,
Melbourne, and Delhi

Editor Daniel Mills
US Editor Charles Wills
Senior Art Editor Helen Spencer
Production Editor Ben Marcus
Production Controller Hema Gohil
Executive Managing Editor Adèle Hayward
Managing Art Editor Kat Mead
Art Director Peter Luff
Publisher Stephanie Jackson

DK DELHI
Editors Saloni Talwar, Rima Zaheer
Designer Tannishtha Chakraborty
Design Manager Arunesh Talapatra
DTP Designer Pushpak Tyagi

First American Edition, 2009

Published in the United States by DK Publishing
375 Hudson Street, New York, New York 10014

09 10 11 12 10 9 8 7 6 5 4 3 2 1

ND137—October 2009

Published in Great Britain by
Dorling Kindersley Limited.

A catalog record for this book is available from
the Library of Congress.

ISBN 978-0-7566-4197-9

DK books are available at special discounts
when purchased in bulk for sales promotions,
premiums, fund-raising, or educational use.
For details, contact: DK Publishing Special Markets,
375 Hudson Street, New York, New York 10014 or
SpecialSales@dk.com.

Color reproduction
by Colorscan, Singapore
Printed in China by WKT

Discover more at **www.dk.com**

Contents

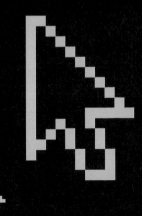

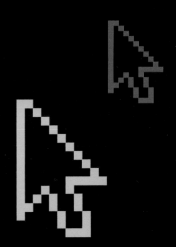

Introduction

The digital revolution has changed—and will continue to change—the way in which customers expect organizations and brands to communicate with them. Bombarding passive customers with one-way marketing is no longer acceptable. Customers want to be in a conversation. They want to be part of the brand. They want a voice—and the Internet has given it to them. The 21st-century manager must adapt to these expectations in order to succeed.

The Digital Revolution aims to provide an insight for managers into this revolutionary new medium, covering the impact of digital media on business in a logical sequence. Readers will be taken through a step-by-step guide to the key issues in the implementation of various on-line strategies and tactics available to the contemporary manager.

With the help of this book, readers will learn about all the key elements of digital media and their impact on management. The organization's website is at the hub of its digital marketing, and has a chapter to itself, but it does not exist in isolation. Digital buying behavior, the social media, search engine optimization, on-line advertising, and e-mail all play an important role in managing an organization in the digital age.

Chapter 1

Making sense of the digital world

Before considering how you and your organization can benefit from digital technology, it is important to understand the environment in which it developed. This includes the history of the technology, and the habits of the people who use it.

Understanding the technology

While it is not vital for you as a manager to fully understand the technology behind digital applications, exploring the background of the digital environment will help you to appreciate the revolution it has driven.

Defining the term "digital"

The term digital describes information that is stored and transmitted in terms of discrete numbers—the distinct seconds and minutes of a digital clock, as opposed to the sweeping hands of an analog device. Digital technology is now used in all "traditional" media, but is most associated with computing and the Internet.

How browsing works

1 STORAGE
The website content sits on its host computer (server).

2 REQUEST
The surfer types a page's URL or clicks on a link to request the content.

The history of the Internet

The Internet*, used by millions around the globe, was conceived by military scientists. Fearing the effects of nuclear attack on conventional communications systems, American leaders during the Cold War instigated the ARPANet (Advanced Research Projects Agency Network) project, a system of computers that would eventually become the Internet. Academics such as Englishman Tim Berners-Lee, known as the "father of the Internet", contributed to its development, and commercial use of the Internet began in 1993, with the launch of the first web browser, Mosaic. Forward-thinking business leaders recognized the potential of this new medium, and its popularity grew. The "dot com" boom at the turn of the 21st century was swiftly followed by the "dot bomb" bust as ill-thought-out digital enterprises rose and fell, but this did not stop the Internet from becoming an integral part of society, business, and government.

*Internet —
The Internet is an inter-network of computers. If you use the world wide web (www) or e-mail, you are using the Internet.

Evaluating the future

Improving technology allows the transmission of ever more complex data. Bandwidth—the amount of data that can be carried by an Internet connection—is constantly increasing, but video and on-line gaming require much greater resources than simple text and images and the system is in danger of overloading. "Net neutrality" may become an important issue in the future as many see the Internet developing into a "two-tier" system, with faster downloading sites costing extra money to host, giving big business the best access.

3 FORWARD
The Internet Service Provider forwards the request to the server.

4 SEND
The server sends the files as a series of packets of data.

5 DELIVER
The data is presented as a web page.

Being in a digital world

Although those within the industry had predicted its coming, for the majority of people, the digital revolution happened comparitively overnight. Where other media like radio and TV took decades to develop and generations to be accepted, the Internet has come from nowhere to become part of our lives in just a few years.

Communicating via the Internet

In the hype that surrounded the Internet in its first decade of life, it is often forgotten that it is primarily a medium that helps people communicate, rather than a panacea for all business and social problems. It is how it is used that makes it effective, efficient, or useful. As a means of carrying a message, personal or commercial, it is faster, more accessible, and more interactive than any other medium. Most importantly, it allows people to communicate with other like-minded individuals or groups around the world. Never before could one person post a message that could be read by anyone, anywhere or everyone, everywhere. As a means of exchanging information the Internet cannot be rivaled—recognize this and use it to communicate effectively with your customers.

Living with the Internet

Apart from its commercial applications the Internet is also used by many as part of their social life; sites that cater to this are part of what has been dubbed the social media. Such sites facilitate chats with friends and acquaintances and discussions on hobbies, and provide a platform for self-help groups to disseminate knowledge or experiences. When we include the influence of the web on our buying decisions, e-mail as 21st-century postal service, and social media as a key element in our social life, it is easy to see why most users consider the Internet vital to their lifestyle.

Taking the bad with the good

No culture is without opportunists, and the digital society has its share of fraudsters and vandals. Even law-abiding citizens may be concerned about the Internet's ability to gather data. The theft of personal information, data collected by marketers to target their advertising, or simply easy access to information in the public domain are all perceived as threats to individual privacy. These concerns affect the consumers' willingness to engage in digital commerce and communications.

 IN FOCUS... NUMBER OF USERS

In regions where the Internet was first adopted, mainly the USA, Northern Europe, and Scandinavia, usage numbers have peaked at around 70 percent of the population. However, these figures are likely to be dwarfed in the near future by the number of users in Asia. So far only around 15 percent of Asia's population have access to the web. There is a divide between those who are on-line and those who aren't, but when densely populated countries like India and China reach 70 percent Internet penetration, users in Asia will far outnumber those in the western world.

Using social media

The greatest impact the digital revolution has had on society is the opening up of personal communication between the masses around the world. Social media ensure that an individual's sphere of interaction is no longer limited to a few friends and acquaintances.

Understanding social media

Although access to contemporary media—newspapers, TV, and radio—is still restricted by their owners, the Internet has provided a platform for individual voices to be heard. That outlet, social media, comes in many forms. The term refers not so much to the actual media but more their content—all of which is freely available for anyone to read, contribute to, and engage with. The other key aspect of social networking is that it is a many-to-many, conversational medium with a complex relationship between audience and sender.

> **SOCIAL NETWORKING**
> You can connect with people on social networking sites. Various applications on these sites enhance the experience.

Recognizing its impact

Citizens of the digital society are more trusting of each other than they are of marketing or corporate messages—something that has prompted commentators to suggest that, in the digital age, the organization no longer has total control of its marketing. However, while freedom from control gives kudos to social media, lack of editorial control means accuracy and quality may be compromised, compared to professionally-produced content.

> **SOCIAL LEARNING**
> You can learn from content generated by others or by experts on some sites. You can even benefit from others' views on various issues.

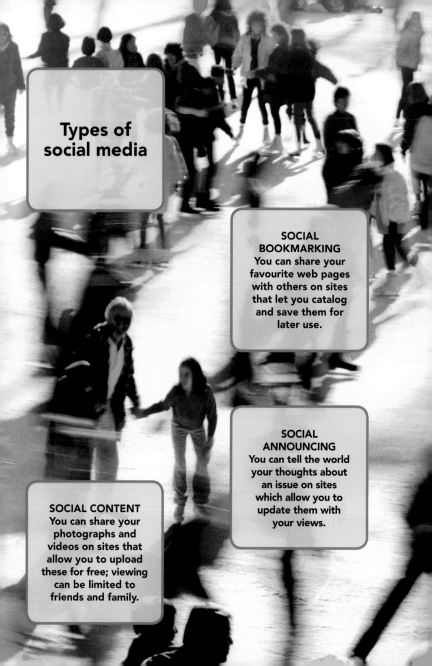

Types of social media

SOCIAL BOOKMARKING
You can share your favourite web pages with others on sites that let you catalog and save them for later use.

SOCIAL ANNOUNCING
You can tell the world your thoughts about an issue on sites which allow you to update them with your views.

SOCIAL CONTENT
You can share your photographs and videos on sites that allow you to upload these for free; viewing can be limited to friends and family.

Using consumers' content

Any element of digital media not developed by professionals is known as consumer generated content (CGC) or user generated content (UGC). In a wider context it is also referred to as consumer generated media (CGM), which reflects its status as part of social media.

HOW TO... BLOG FOR BUSINESS

Identify the objectives and target audience.

↓

Plan the content so it meets those objectives.

↓

Decide on a name for the blog that will reflect its content.

↓

Open an account on a blog-hosting website.

↓

Inform your audience of your blog's existence.

↓

Update it with interesting content regularly.

Communicating amateur content

UGC developers (sometimes called citizen journalists) can communicate their thoughts on digital media in three formats: text, audio, and video. The popular website YouTube has made web video a much publicized format. Audio comes by way of podcasts—though these are often simply spoken versions of written content. Just as YouTube has made amateur videos popular, MySpace and Facebook have given a platform to digital citizens to write their own web content. These sites are a symbol of social media in that their pages are a place where members socialize with their friends, associates, and even strangers. Those who are not satisfied with using the web to share files can write their own blog (a contraction of the term weblog). These function as on-line journals, often used to share opinions and commentary.

Using CGC commercially

Individuals and organizations have realized that CGC platforms can be used for marketing messages. For example, YouTube now shows professionally-produced videos. Similarly, some of the most popular blogs are written by experts in their field. Although some of these people blog for altruistic reasons, most use the medium to promote themselves, their businesses, or their employers.

Benefiting from reviews

If maintaining a blog is too much for some, there is another, much easier way for business to attract opinions on-line—by completing on-line reviews. For some websites, publishing review forums is a business model that generates income by selling on-site advertising. Others use reviews as additional content to attract visitors—many people like to learn about other users' own experiences regarding a product or service, while on-line retailers treat customer reviews as part of their sales copy for products they are promoting. Amazon, for example, encourages people to review books, while eBay solicits feedback on how well sellers perform. Research suggests that over 60 percent of off-line customers check on-line reviews, blogs, and other on-line customer feedback before they consider purchasing a new product or service.

As a digital manager you need to be aware of what is written about your organization on various on-line forums. This is not only a convenient way to get feedback; you can take quick action if you find too many negative opinions are making the rounds.

TIP

ENCOURAGE FEEDBACK

Make it simple for users to leave comments on your web content or blog. For example, a clickable star or a simple thumbs-up image will save them having to type in their opinion.

IN FOCUS... CITIZEN MARKETERS

Most contributors to social media websites pass judgements on an organization, product, or brand and their comments can be postive or negative depending on how satisfied they were with it. The most enthusiastic supporters are known as citizen marketers. Where consumer generated content has the capacity to be negative and critical, citizen marketers are satisfied customers who give only positive reviews. This can be taken to such an extreme that the writer actually sets out to promote the subject of their comments and so can be considered to be producing marketing and advertising content on behalf of the subject. They can be called the voice of the digital fan club, and since a lot of customers tend to check reviews on-line, citizen marketers can prove to be quite helpful to an organization.

Communicating digitally

Whether it is a business, a public entity, or a non-profit association, it is now impossible for an organization to function without using digital technology in its external and internal communications. The digital organization needs to facilitate personal communications with three key groups: its staff, its suppliers, and its customers.

Bringing your staff closer

Prior to the digital revolution, one-to-one communication between members of staff was restricted to land-line telephones and face-to-face conversations. Traveling staff such as salespeople could spend the week on the road with little or no contact with their managers or suppliers, making it much harder to adapt strategies and discuss deals in real time. They would also feel less "connected" to their organization. Today, whether using desk-bound or mobile facilities, the modern worker is never out of touch with base— no matter what the distance is in miles—thanks to the ready availability of cell phones, laptops, hand-held devices, and wi-fi (wireless networking technology). Easy access to mobile communication greatly adds to the effectiveness and efficiency of staff, no matter where they work in the organization, and providing it should be a high priority for any manager in the digital age.

CASE STUDY

The reach of the Internet

One company that has benefited hugely from advances in digital communications is UK-based 4Projects. Before the advent of digital telecommunications, project managers on remote construction sites were reliant on driving miles over rough terrain to contact suppliers and central offices. 4Projects developed an Internet-based project management service, which can also be operated through mobile Internet connections, to address this problem for its clients. Improved communications with remote sites allow substantial savings of time and money, and 4Projects software is now used by over 100,000 people across five continents.

Making logistics simple for suppliers

Digital communication also improves the efficiency of procurement, storage, and distribution strategies. While contact between individuals is still a key aspect of efficient operations, digital technology has also made strategic management far more efficient. Computer programs are used to track and control processes such as stock management and delivery schedules, with global positioning locating the whereabouts of orders at any given time. Furthermore, Electronic Product Codes (EPC) using Radio Frequency Identification (RFID) scanners facilitate the control of inventory, storage, and logistics, as well as aiding electronic point of sale (EPOS) systems.

Communicating with your customers

Digital technology has made communication within an organization and contact with external suppliers both convenient and less expensive, but using it to interact with your customers is where it can generate income for the organization.

Although personal contact is common in business-to-business (B2B) environments, it is in consumer marketing that digital technology has had the greatest impact. Digital facilities like e-mail and chat, and the interactive nature of many websites, allow personal relationships to develop between vendor and customer in a way that was not possible using traditional mass communications media.

✔ CHECKLIST **MAKING THE MOST OF DIGITAL CONNECTIVITY**

	YES	NO
• Do you use SMS to address urgent issues?	☐	☐
• Do you use e-mails to allow messages to be sent and opened at the sender's and receiver's convenience?	☐	☐
• Do you discuss issues via video conferences, which are cost saving and have less of an impact on the environment than travel?	☐	☐
• Do you use cell phones so that you can reach essential contacts, and be reached by them, at any time?	☐	☐

Digital buying behavior

The impact of the digital revolution on society is particularly evident in the way contemporary consumers make purchase decisions. Gone are the days when customers were limited to a few local stores—the digital shopper can now access product information at home, at the workplace, or, if they have access to mobile devices, virtually anywhere.

Understanding buyer behavior

*Buying cycle —
a series of actions comprising problem recognition, information search, evaluation of alternatives, and purchase decision.

Buyers go through a process called the buying cycle* during which they address their purchasing needs. This concept suggests that each purchase is made up of a series of actions that determine the final decision. A further step is that of post-purchase behavior— often considered to be a psychological justification for the purchase that reinforces the buying decision.

Changing buyer behavior

Digital media has revolutionized buying behavior by making huge amounts of information readily available to the buyer. On-line retailers now publish information about their products in greater detail than traditional media, and more economically. However, as in traditional media, this information is marketing copy designed to sell the product. While this information can be useful to the potential buyer, it is independent on-line information that tends to be most valued by the consumer. This is now easily available on regulated watchdog-type websites, review sites, and individual blogs.

Sourcing digital information

There are three key attractions to using digital information in making purchase decisions:

• **Independent data** Independent reviews are much easier to find on-line. Research suggests that buyers trust content that is generated independently more than business websites advertising a product.

• **Convenience** Buyers can go through every stage of the buying cycle from the comfort of their armchair, from researching alternatives to making a purchase and having it delivered to their home.

• **Lower prices** Lower business start-up and operating costs, combined with numerous price-comparison websites and wider product availability, make it easy for consumers to track down the lowest prices for the product or service they are interested in.

COMPARING CONVENTIONAL AND DIGITAL BUYING CYCLES

TASKS	PRE-DIGITAL	USING DIGITAL TECHNOLOGY
Problem recognition	• Your roses are dying and gardening books have no mention of the disease	• You find out in a gardening chat room that a parasite, new to the region, is infecting your roses
Information search	• Members of your local gardening club are unable to offer a solution	• You join a gardening group on a social media website to discuss your problem
Evaluation of alternatives	• You are told that the horticultural show taking place next month is your last hope to find out more	• You decide on a particular product that is highly recommended by gardeners on several review websites
Purchase decision	• You are unaware of a solution, let alone which product to buy	• You order the product from an on-line gardening shop
Post-purchase behaviour	• You have not progressed	• You post your comments about the product on review sites

Chapter 2

Marketing to an on-line audience

For the vast majority of organizations, digital elements are now an indispensible part of their marketing and communications efforts. Although some organizations find digital technology challenging, no organization can afford to ignore it.

Integrating digital marketing

It is important for the contemporary marketer to appreciate that not only should digital be included as a basic element of the marketing mix* but that digital has a mix of its own. Digital marketing will only be effective if it is developed as carefully as traditional marketing.

Incorporating digital marketing

*Marketing mix — *a model that describes marketing as a combination of product, promotion, price, and placement, known as the 4Ps, which must be balanced in order to market a product, brand, or organization.*

Very often, organizations make the mistake of using digital media in isolation and not integrating it with off-line marketing efforts. To be effective, all marketing—no matter what the medium—must be coordinated. A lack of integration causes a conflict between traditional and digital media. In the end, the decision on integration is made for organizations by their customers—the digital-savvy 21st-century consumer expects digital and traditional marketing to connect. And if you are not able to offer them integrated marketing options, they will take their business elsewhere.

Combining digital elements

Although a website is the focal point of any on-line marketing effort, it cannot function effectively in isolation from the other elements of the digital marketing mix. To make the best use of the various digital elements available, you must use them in combination. Direct marketing e-mails, for example, should maximize their interactive nature by including a link to the organization's web presence, as should responses on customer review sites, and any viral campaign should, ultimately, drive users to a web page. By the same token, a website can be where the e-marketing efforts originate—with visitors interacting with on-site messages or promotions such as games or virtual environments, on-line worlds inhabited by the alter egos of real people.

TIP

USE INFLUENCE
Invite influential bloggers to post reviews of your organization's products or services.

Using interactivity

No other medium allows a viewer, reader, or listener to instantly express an interest in a product, seek more information about it, and even buy it, at the touch of a button. It is the interactive nature of digital media that lends its various elements so readily to being seamlessly integrated in the marketing process. Sales models and practices focus on taking the customer on a smooth path from interest to action. This is problematic when the path involves multi-media experiences. For example, a radio advertisement giving a phone number for customers to call for more information gives latitude for them to step (or fall) off the path. Digital communications, on the other hand, can allow a surfer to read about a product in an e-mail, click on a link to a website, research the product specifications, watch a video showing it in action, read what other customers have to say, and then place an order on-line.

HOW TO...
INTEGRATE ON- AND OFF-LINE MARKETING

Update your website as you launch your product.

⬇

Leak an advance screening of your product's TV advertisement on-line.

⬇

Release insider blogs on your product's capabilities.

⬇

Place advertisements on digital TV, utilizing the interactive element.

⬇

Be on top of the search engine listings for the product's name and tag line.

⬇

Send e-mails urging customers to go to the website or a physical outlet.

⬇

Encourage consumer-generated reviews on social media sites.

⬇

Place infomercials in local newspapers with contact details for the local dealer.

⬇

Facilitate on-line registrations for a product preview.

⬇

Take on-line orders for the product, and have it delivered or picked up.

Using search plus

Around two-thirds of all search engine enquiries have an off-line influence—and as a digital marketer you must not only optimize your on-line presence to benefit from those stimuli, but also be proactive in predicting the keywords. A keyword is a word or phrase entered into a search engine in order to find websites that include content related to that keyword. Predicting the keywords that customers will take from off-line marketing allows you to purchase appropriate keyword-driven advertising. Integrating on-line search results with advertising in other mediums in this way is called "search plus". For example, search plus:

• **television** Commercials and product placements can cause search spikes for relevant phrases.

• **outdoor advertising** Commuters might only get a glimpse of a billboard advertisement, and may want to search for further details on-line.

• **public relations** Pertinent keywords can be purchased to dispel rumours or provide a response to negative press.

• **direct mail** Receivers of postal mailings seek further information on the promoted product or service, and the brand message is reinforced if it appears high in the search engine results.

Tracking user information

One of the key advantages of digital media is that on-line, users always leave a digital footprint of where they have been, where they came from, how often they visit, when they last visited, what they looked at but didn't buy and—hopefully—what they eventually purchased. Such data can be stored, mined, and analyzed to create information that is useful to the organization. This can be generic (for example, marketing intelligence such as which sites send most customers to your website) or it can be personal to the individual user. As long as they are made aware of what you are doing—and preferably agree to it—users can be tagged with cookies, electronic calling cards left on a user's computer to facilitate the recording of data about the user and their visit(s) to the website that issued the cookie. This is done so that information about their interactions with the site can be used in the future to provide the customer with a better service.

CASE STUDY

How cookies help sell books

One effective practitioner in the use of cookies is Amazon. Cookies left on computers during previous visits mean that customers returning to their web pages are presented with advertisements that are contextualized with products viewed, searches completed, and products purchased while they surfed the site. Also, the actual content of the user's "homepage" can be personalized based on the information retained on the cookies. For example, the software can analyze books that the user has shown interest in, or bought, previously, and offer a list of "recommended books" based on the authors or subjects of those texts.

Retailing by bricks and clicks

Integrating on- and off-line marketing is vital in the retail sector. Bricks-and-clicks retailers sell in both physical stores (bricks) and on-line (clicks). As a digital manager you can integrate both offerings to suit the needs of even the most demanding of your customers.

WATCH THE LAW
Consumer protection legislation differs from country to country, so make sure your multi-channel efforts do not run foul of any laws—particularly if you deliver products around the world.

Debunking channel conflict

In the early days of the commercial Internet, most traditional "bricks" retailers were reluctant to join the digital revolution. Even those who understood more about the web were afraid to adopt it as part of their sales and distribution chain. The worry was that every on-line sale would be one lost from the physical store—leading to so-called "channel conflict." The result was, of course, that competitors who had adopted the Internet gained with on-line sales—and the off-line company lost out both ways. With on-line sales fast approaching 20 percent of all retail, many predict an imminent "tipping point" when all retailers will invest in multi-channel selling and the proportion of on-line sales will rise higher still.

Integrating on- and off-line shopping

Customers are no longer content to travel to an outlet, buy a product, and carry it home. Digital-age customers may want the flexibility to "click and collect"—pay for an item on-line and collect it from the store. There are three drivers for this: saving shipping expenses, convenience, and meeting an immediate need. Customer demands have increased—but so have the opportunities for the digitally aware retailer to meet those demands.

Meeting customers' expectations

Many cross-channel customers, who use both on- and off-line methods to shop, not only want to be able to walk into the store after surfing the Internet and purchase or pick up the perfect product, they expect the store to be aware of their order and have it ready and waiting. But the expectation doesn't end there. If they order clothes on-line and discover on delivery that they don't fit, they expect to be able to return them to a local store. The customers might even want to send a text message to check if the right size is available before driving down to the shops. Many commentators have suggested that the day of the single transaction is dead and the future of marketing is in developing relationships with customers, so ensuring future sales. If that is the case, then effective multi-channel retailing strategies will have a big say in the success—or otherwise—of maintaining those relationships.

? ASK YOURSELF... CAN I GET ON-LINE CUSTOMERS TO MY PHYSICAL STORE?

- Do I advertise price promotions on-line that are only available in-store?
- Do I inform my on-line customers when I have in-store events, such as book signings or food preparation demonstrations?
- Do I offer discount coupons that can be printed at home but which are redeemable only at my store?
- Do I inform my on-line shoppers about my physical store's refits or upgrades? On-line only shoppers may be unaware of such improvements.

TIP

CHOOSE YOUR OUTSOURCERS CAREFULLY
If you are outsourcing your delivery, make sure you pick a partner that shares your customer service standards. If their goods don't arrive, customers blame the website that took the order, not the delivery company.

Managing fulfillment

It doesn't matter how good your website is, how wide a range of products it lists, or how competitive its prices are if the goods do not arrive at the right address and at a time that is convenient to the buyer.

However, effective fulfillment starts before the product is dispatched from the distribution center. Stock-control systems can be linked to the website so that on-line buyers can check the availability of products before they order. Delivery schedules as well as the costs of standard and premium shipping options can be detailed on the website. For low-cost items, an e-mail can inform a customer when goods have been shipped. For high-value products, delivery companies can provide on-line tracking so that customers can follow the progress of their order from the warehouse to their front door.

IN FOCUS...
USING INTERACTIVITY TO ITS BEST EFFECT

Traditional sales models focus on taking the customer on a smooth path from interest in a product or service, to action (usually a purchase). Off-line, that path can be blocked by unplanned obstacles—but on-line the buyer can move from expressing an interest in a product, to seeking more information about it, and then to buying it, all at the click of a mouse. Using the interactive nature of digital media and combining it with high quality fulfillment can ensure that the various elements of that path are seamlessly integrated, helping to convert interested browsers into purchasing customers.

Giving customers satisfaction

As with all marketing problems, the answer to just how multi-channel you should be lies with the customers. If they expect that there will be a click-and-collect service or an in-store returns and exchange facility then you must provide them. Sales is at the sharp-end of the firm's relationship with its customers, so keep yourself up-to-date about the services that your competitors are offering and make sure your organization does not lag behind.

Retailing intangible products

It easy to forget that "retail" also includes the sale of intangible goods or services—and yet it is in this field that perhaps the majority of on-line sales value lies. The selling price of a single on-line vacation booking, for example, would equate to hundreds of book purchases. Such transactions can also lead to multi-channel exposure—for example, the customer might want to collect the travel documents from a physical store rather than wait for them to arrive by post. A further consideration for service providers, such as hairstylists and opticians, is to allow customers to make appointments on-line—making your booking office open 24/7. Practised effectively, the costs of necessary software can be offset by staff not having to answer phone calls from customers seeking detailed information. You can also use the booking web page of your website to up-sell (offering upgrades and other add-ons to the original product or service) and cross-sell (selling an additional product or service). These value add-ons for customers could be in the form of a service contract, an extended warranty, insurance, or installation services.

TIP

OFFER EXTRA SERVICE

Have an express delivery option on your e-commerce website for customers with urgent needs.

✔ **CHECKLIST BEING A MULTI-CHANNEL RETAILER**

	YES	NO
• Can your customers visit an outlet, view products, and then make a purchase at home via the Internet?	☐	☐
• Can they select a product on your website, purchase it on-line, and collect it from an outlet, or pay after having it delivered?	☐	☐
• Can they text an order via cell phone to reserve a product?	☐	☐
• Can they buy a product using any method described above and then have it gift-wrapped and delivered to a third-party's address?	☐	☐

Marketing on social media

Traditional media have always been channels for marketing messages; indeed, many media outlets are funded by advertising. In this respect, social media is no different—but its users are. They value the honesty of "people like us" in consumer-generated content and they do not like to be misled. Social media is "for the people, by the people" not "from the marketer."

TIP

KEEP AN EYE ON THE OPPOSITION
As well as tracking what people are saying about you—keep an eye open for comments about your competitors as well. Negative or positive, they can be useful for your own marketing.

Gaining market information

In traditional market research, members of the public answer questions about what they think of an organization, brand, or product. This method is flawed as it is difficult to gauge what respondents really think, and it is also expensive. Now, as part of any marketing intelligence strategy, researchers can see what customers honestly think by reading their reviews and comments on social media sites. Instead of trawling the web, you can use software to inform you whenever your organization, brand, or product name is searched for on Google or entered into a blog.

Involving yourself

While passive viewing of social media sites can provide valuable information, marketers can also be proactive. Your organization can get involved in the various review, blog, and community sites. For example, you can respond to negative reviews by adding a comment that the problem has now been resolved, or go to chat rooms, forums, and blogs, and engage in the digital conversation. You have to decide whether or not to declare your interest. It is better to be up-front about your connection to the product before giving advice. Otherwise you risk being exposed, and losing credibility in a valuable market niche.

Advertising on social networks

Social media sites have a particular appeal for advertisers, but there is a significant drawback. Many participants visit community sites to escape the commercial environment in which they live, and so tend to "blank-out" any advertisements that might appear on the pages. To get around this, you will need to make your advertisement relevant to the contributor. Digital technology can help you by matching keywords in the advertisements to the content of the web page, so that the advertisements presented can be matched to the subject of the discussion. For example, if the forum discussion is about a particular movie star, the advertisements might include their biography and DVDs of their films.

TIP

CREATE A FAN PAGE

Set up a fan page on a social media site where satisfied customers can leave messages of support—it may attract new customers to your organization or product.

Choosing social marketing options

	YOU CONTROL	OTHERS CONTROL
TWO-WAY WEB	**HOME WEB 2** Sites on which communication with customers is two-way, but is controlled by the organization. This consists mainly of the organization's own social media content.	**EXTENDED WEB 2** Sites over which organizations have no control, and consumers interact with each independently. These form the core of social media.
ONE-WAY WEB	**HOME WEB 1** Sites on which the marketer controls the message and communication is one-way, from retailer to consumer. A retailer's website is one example.	**EXTENDED WEB 1** Sites on which organizations can place content but do not control it. Advertising on social media and community sites falls under this category.

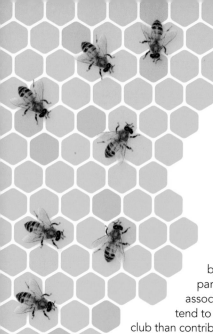

Building your own community

Almost by definition, social media sites are organic—developed and grown by people who have a genuine interest in the subject. Sometimes these communities are dedicated to an organization or brand, and although they act as marketing conduits, their origins lie in high levels of customer satisfaction. Some brands develop their own virtual community by setting up custom sites or dedicating part of their web presence to activities associated with social media. Participants tend to see themselves more as members of a club than contributors to an independent social site. In marketing terms, these enterprises are more an aspect of relationship marketing than they are social media.

TIP

BE HONEST IN YOUR BLOG

Blogs that feign impartiality but are actually promotional messages are known as "flogs". They are easily spotted and can drive customers away. On-line, honesty is the best policy.

Using commercial blogs

For some organizations—or individuals—publishing their own blog can be an effective element of a branding strategy. Practiced properly, the commercial blog can be advantageous in developing consumer relationships. An enterprise of any size can maintain a blog, but the key lies in producing something of value to the reader. For example, Google has a blog, written by one of its chief engineers, that tells users how Google's search algorithm works and gives tips on optimization. A small business might have expertise or experience in a B2B niche market, and a blog on this subject could be used to attract practitioners and customers. A consultant can also use a considered blog as a showcase of their expertise.

Understanding viral marketing

The digital version of word-of-mouth marketing, viral marketing, relies on individuals to pass on the marketing message to their friends and acquaintances. A variety of digital channels can be used to pass the message, with social media the most common. While traditional word-of-mouth campaigns rely heavily on providing an exceptional service which customers will (hopefully) relay to others, for a viral campaign to be successful you must offer some motivation for the customer to pass the message on. This could be a tangible reward such as a free gift, or an intangible reward such as the kudos the sender will receive from friends for sharing it. The message must also be something people want to talk about—something that creates a buzz.

TIP

CREATE A BUZZ
Viral marketing only works if consumers want to pass on your message. Where they may not be willing to share a straightforward marketing message, something entertaining or unusual is much more likely to be circulated. Funny or controversial content is usually best for this.

USING VIRAL MARKETING

⬆ FAST TRACK	❗ OFF TRACK
Developing two or more 20-second videos and giving them exciting titles	Developing a two-minute video and making it obvious that it is an advertisement
Putting the clips on several social media sites	Putting the clip only on one social media site
Making sure the thumbnails are appealing	Allowing the site to choose a random image as the thumbnail
Being proactive and e-mailing all your contacts asking them to comment, give feedback, or simply discuss the entries	Waiting passively for reactions and not encouraging an exchange of views

Using digital public relations

Public and press relations—the practice of, and methods employed in, creating, promoting, or maintaining goodwill and a favorable image among the public for an organization, institution, brand, individual, or product—were once separate (though related) disciplines, but the digital age has seen them draw closer together.

Understanding digital press

In the pre-Internet era, public relations (PR) staff or agents would covet a relationship with key journalists who would decide how and when the public might read a press release. In the digital age, however, the release of information can be made directly to the general public. Furthermore by using social media, that same public can share the information around the globe in a matter of minutes. There are some on-line writers and bloggers who can make or break a story by commenting on it or ignoring it.

BIOGRAPHIES
Including short profiles and photographs of key personnel, and up-to-date contact details of PR personnel.

Managing your reputation

It is in a crisis that digital PR is most helpful. Your website is likely to be the first destination for people seeking information, and you can now put an immediate, detailed response to a crisis on-line for all to see. Digital media also makes it easier for dissatisfied customers to voice their anger. A blog grievance can develop into a "cyberbashing" site, dedicated to publicizing your failings. Legal measures usually attract further bad press, and a better response in such cases is to start a dialog with unhappy individuals before problems escalate.

LOGOS
Making digital versions of the company logo available to be printed alongside positive news stories.

Elements of a digital press kit

PHOTO LIBRARY
Uploading a photo library of the staff, head office, manufacturing centers, etc.

LOCATION DETAILS
Providing details of the locations as well as contact numbers of all company offices.

EVENT INFORMATION
Showcasing audio and video clips of events that emphasize the strengths of the organization.

PRODUCT DESCRIPTIONS
Giving detailed information with images of all products or services your organization offers.

Using an e-marketplace

In trading, a marketplace is where sellers interact with buyers, and this definition could also be applied to the web. However, in the digital world the term e-marketplace is most commonly used for websites that link buyers and suppliers electronically to automate corporate procurement.

TIP

BE VISIBLE

Join more than one e-marketplace. One for each segment of the market in which you trade is a good start.

Exploiting the e-marketplace

The Internet, and especially e-marketplaces, have had a huge impact on the B2B environment. The strength of a traditional marketplace is judged by how far traders travel to it. For the digital market this distance can be global, making the e-marketplace an infinitely stronger proposition. On-line, the smallest business can compete against the biggest. E-marketplaces are also a place to network. They provide a focal point for owners, managers, and workers to communicate with suppliers or customers. Do not ignore appropriate e-marketplaces or you risk isolating yourself from the industry.

Understanding e-auctions

Although B2B on-line marketplaces make straightforward exchanges possible by providing a digital shop window for vendors to advertise and buyers to browse, the focus of many e-marketplaces tends to be on-line auctions, both forward and reverse. The forward auction allows potential buyers to bid against each other for an advertised product, which goes to the highest bidder.In reverse auctions, the buyer initiates bids, the intention being to drive the purchase price down. Auctions in the digital age allow buyers and sellers around the world to track and take part in multiple auctions using dedicated software to manage bids and sales.

Tendering on-line

In government procurement, tendering is used to find suppliers for everything from military aircraft to paperclips, and is a serious element of many companies' marketing efforts. However, traditional tendering was complex and time consuming, and only major industry players could devote the resources to track, develop, and submit tenders. This is not the case with the on-line tender. Now, a one-time registration with the relevant authorities means that an e-mail lets you know of suitable jobs, with on-line application also alleviating repetition in submissions. Furthermore, the e-tendering systems of many public sector entities facilitate joint tenders, allowing small businesses to combine their capabilities for a single bid, and partial bids, where you allow others to bid for the outstanding elements of the contract.

TIP

MAKE A FIRST E-IMPRESSION

Carefully prepare your application details before applying to join an e-marketplace. Your credibility depends on how you present your company and product details.

PROFITING FROM THE E-MARKETPLACE

 FAST TRACK

 OFF TRACK

FAST TRACK	OFF TRACK
Being selective with the e-marketplace you register with	Registering with many, but then rarely visiting them
Making your organization and your products appealing on the registration form	Filling in the bare details of your organization or products on the registration form
Participating in discussions and offering advice	Joining in only when you think an order might result
Tracking "calls for tender" consistently	Checking tender information only occasionally

Chapter 3

Creating an effective web presence

An organization's web presence is the most important aspect of its digital marketing effort. The corporate website is often the first point of contact for both customers and suppliers who are seeking information about an organization.

Defining objectives

In marketing and communications, there are just three objectives for any website: brand development, revenue generation, and customer service or support. Although a website can address all these, one aspect must take precedence—the site's primary objective.

Branding through the website

*Channel conflict —
Where multiple methods of distribution conflict with each other. For example, a manufacturer selling goods directly to customers as well as through retailers.

The brand-development website is used to compliment the organization's off-line branding. Significantly—particularly in the B2C environment—it offers no on-line purchase facility. It is mostly used by manufacturers who use other channels of distribution for sales and wish to avoid channel conflict*. Increasingly, potential customers use the web to check out organizations of all kinds, from local schools to multinational corporations, and first impressions last. Your website must, therefore, be an integral element of the organization's branding strategy.

Generating revenue

This type of site increases revenue through sales, lead generation, or direct marketing, making return on investment (ROI) easy to assess. While it is B2C online purchasing that courts publicity, B2B transactions will always dwarf B2C sales. On-line purchasing is not feasible for most B2B products, therefore the B2B website is designed to present buyers with information and content that will prompt them to contact the vendor.

TIP

THINK ABOUT OBJECTIVES

When developing a site, ask yourself: What are its objectives? Who will visit it? Why will they be visiting?

Providing customer service

Digital communications, when used properly, enhance the service and support offered to customers effectively and at significantly reduced costs. The Internet has developed into an indispensible source of information and it is hard to imagine a life without it. Whether a customer is searching for a lost instruction manual or an airline's flight schedule, in the digital era these can be made easily available on-line. Similarly, you can carefully develop a FAQ page on your organization's website that addresses those issues that generate repeated queries from customers.

✔ **CHECKLIST KEEPING THE WEBSITE'S OBJECTIVES IN MIND**

	YES	NO
• Have you discussed goals with developers, so they can use appropriate technology, presentation style, and brand aesthetics?	☐	☐
• Have you set objectives against which you can measure the effectiveness of the site?	☐	☐
• Have you assessed the ROI for any expenditure on the website against its objectives?	☐	☐

Getting started

The organization's website should be a considered undertaking, and before any steps are taken in its actual design and development a number of key issues must be addressed: who is responsible for it, on what domain name it will sit, and where it will be hosted.

TIP

GAIN E-MAIL CREDIBILITY

Use an e-mail address based in your own domain name to establish yourself—people don't trust a business that uses a personal e-mail account like @yahoo.

Addressing management issues

Appoint someone to manage the development and maintenance of your organization's website. In a small business it might be a single person, but in larger organizations it is likely that a number of people—both internal and external—will be required. In this case, put one person in overall charge of the project. Do not make the mistake of leaving website development in the hands of the IT department. Make sure someone with editorial and marketing experience is in charge.

IN FOCUS...
DOMAIN NAME CONSTRUCTION

The primary domain is the last part of the Internet domain name. For a top-level domain (TLD) name such as www.example.com, **www** is the third-level domain, **example** is the second-level domain, and **com** is the primary domain. For a Country Code Top Level Domain (ccTLD) such as www.example.co.uk, **www** is the fourth-level domain, **example** is the third-level, **co** is the second-level, and **uk** is the primary domain, which is reserved for the country.

Getting the right domain name

Often referred to as your address on the web, domain name selection is a strategic marketing decision. In the case of the purely on-line player, it also serves as the brand name of that business. If you have an off-line business that is moving on-line, simply registering the organization's name as a domain is usually the best thing to do, as this will replicate any existing off-line brand value and avoid customer confusion.

Getting the right suffix on your domain name is far from straightforward, but a good rule of thumb is that if you trade only in your country, use its suffix and if you trade globally, use a dot com. There are, however, exceptions to this rule—for US companies, the dot com is both local and global. The use of so-called "novelty" suffixes such as .cc or .biz is not advisable for commercial entities.

Choosing a host for your website

Websites are hosted on computers that are permanently on-line—known as servers. The cost and expertise required means that few organizations operate their own servers, instead outsourcing their website hosting to companies that rent out web space on their servers. Unless you are a serious on-line business, using one of these Internet service providers (ISPs) is the best option. When choosing an ISP, check: the website download speed, the frequency of server downtime, and any security issues regarding the server. Another issue—IP* integrity—relates to how well the server is trusted by e-mail systems and search engines.

*IP (Internet Protocol) — *The Internet Protocol (IP) is a protocol used for transmitting data across the Internet. It is effectively the Internet's operating system.*

ASK YOURSELF... **IS MY DOMAIN NAME APPROPRIATE?**

- Is length an issue? Shorter domain names are generally better.
- How easy will it be for customers to recall the name?
- How will it be communicated—verbally or in print? Can its pronunciation mislead people who are searching for the site?
- Is the domain name the name of the brand and/or business?
- For what purpose is it to be used—website, e-mail address, or company name?

Developing the website

Although it might be possible for an individual to develop a website—and this is often the case, particularly with small businesses—this is not a good idea if the site is to meet its objectives. An effective website requires a number of skill sets to combine in order to meet the needs of its visitors—the organization's customers.

HOW TO... DEVELOP YOUR SITE

Determine the proposed site's objectives.

↓

Register a suitable domain name and rent some web space.

↓

Appoint a website manager.

↓

Decide whether development should be in-house or out-sourced.

↓

Hire specialists to develop the different types of content.

Assembling a "dream team"

Whether the task is completed in-house, or is outsourced in part or completely, a successful website needs input from a range of expertise. Left to their own devices, technicians and designers have a tendency to create sites that are little more than a forum for them to exhibit their design and technical skills with little regard for the website's visitors. Marketers, on the other hand, focus on customers but lack the requisite technical skills to make the site work. A website "dream team" therefore should include: programmers, graphic designers, usability experts, content writers, copy writers, search engine optimization (SEO) specialists, and marketers. Furthermore, for e-commerce sites, the experience of off-line sales staff should not be ignored—they know customers' needs better than anyone else in this list.

Addressing non-technical issues

The art of website development is in the presentation of the content in a way that not only appeals to the target audience, but encourages them to take action that will both meet their needs and the objectives of the site. For the e-commerce site, this means the content performs the duties of a sales person, for the airline site those of the call-centre operative, and so on.

Addressing technical issues

A website is made up of source code that is written by programmers. Similarly text and image appearing on-line must be formatted appropriately by designers. However, not every surfer uses the same equipment to access the site—and as this is beyond the control of the developer it is a significant problem. Technical issues that need to be addressed during development include such things as which browser is being used—Internet Explorer, Firefox, and Safari might read the source code differently, for example. Download speeds will vary depending on the broadband or dial-up facility used. The specification of the users PC or laptop will also come into the equation, as will the software that has been installed on it. Web pages can also format differently on various computer screens.

TEST, TEST, AND TEST AGAIN

Throughout the development of your website, test all technical and non-technical elements before the website goes live.

DESIGNING YOUR HOMEPAGE

FAST TRACK	OFF TRACK
Making sure your homepage downloads quickly	Overloading the homepage with big images or flash-type technology
Using a style that will appeal to your target audience	Ignoring your market segment and keeping your content general
Getting to the point quickly and offering a value proposition	Using self-serving statements like mission objectives
Inspiring visitors to go deeper into the site	Not having clear links to information that the visitor is seeking

Making it easier for customers

If you visited a retail outlet and spent 15 minutes walking around in a vain attempt to find what you came in for, you would be unlikely to become a customer. The store's navigation and usability would have failed, and these two attributes are equally valid—and important—on-line.

TIP

TAKE YOUR CUSTOMERS' POINT OF VIEW
You and your design team should develop the site in such a way that it is easy for everyone to find their way around it. Do not assume that because you can, your customers can too.

Surfing the website

As with any direction-finding exercise, on-line navigation refers to the ease with which visitors find their way around your website. Remember that many visitors will find your site using a search engine, so they might not arrive on the site's home page. This makes it essential for the navigation to be clear on every page—otherwise potential customers might simply click away from your site. The various pages and sections that make up the site should be signposted clearly on an unambiguous contents list.

Making the site user-friendly

Although closely related to navigation, usability takes a more holistic view of website performance. Essentially, website usability is all about how easy it is for a visitor to achieve their objectives for visiting the site. This means making the site simple to use, and since simplicity rarely equates to cutting-edge design, this could result in friction between the designer and the marketer. However, the deciding factor must always be your customers—your site should be designed for them and no one else.

Using the sales funnel

If navigation and usability are important for all sites, for e-commerce sites they are crucial. The site should lead the customer on a path from entry to sale. This path can be seen as a funnel, with customers entering at its widest part (attention*) and exiting at the spout (action). Customers entering further down the funnel (interest or desire) should still be directed to the action stage. The sales funnel can help identify where visitors exit without making a purchase, highlighting flaws in the design.

*Attention — The first stage in the AIDA marketing cycle. A product first attracts the customer's Attention, then their Interest, then the Desire to purchase it, and finally the Action of making a purchase.

ASK YOURSELF... DOES MY SITE CATER TO ALL VISITORS?

- Do I help casual visitors—who don't know what they're looking for but think I might have it—with clear navigation to tell them they're on the right site?
- Do I help visitors who know what they want by supplying comprehensive listings and an in-site search facility to help them find what they want?
- Do I make it easy for customers who know what they want by providing "one-click" navigation to help them find and buy what they want as quickly as possible?

Developing content

There are three key decisions to be made in developing a site's content: First, how to satisfy the need that has brought a visitor to your website; second, what information does the target market expect to be given to help them meet that need; and finally, how do they expect that information to be presented.

TIP

PAY ATTENTION TO CONTENT
Remember that website visitors are there for the content. Good content might overcome basic design, but excessive design won't disguise poor content.

Incorporating text

Pictures might well say a thousand words, but on-line it is usually the textual content, words, that meet the visitors' needs. As well as providing a reason for them being on your site—a unique value proposition is good—the text must be easy to read on a computer screen. Users rarely (if ever) read the contents of a web page, they "scan" it, seeking out key terms or words that they think will help in their information search. To this end, website text should be presented in bite-size chunks—paragraphs with spaces between them, and each with a header to summarize its contents. Dividing the content into sections also helps break continuous text—again, with titles and headers for each segment and sub-division. Finally, use the technology that is unique to the web as a medium of communication—the hyperlink. A printed page is linear: each word, sentence, and page leads you to the next. On-line, however, a sentence or single word, in the form of a hyperlink, can prompt the reader to click away to another page to find the information that they are seeking.

CASE STUDY

Video makes good content
The inclusion of video content is excellent if it is in context to the subject. Two good examples of its use come from Wine Library (www.winelibrary.com) and Intel (www.intel.com). While Intel uses a series of videos to demonstrate its commitment to corporate social responsibility—using an interesting TV-magazine format to give a personal feel, Wine Library has a video of their Director of operations demonstrating his enthusiasm and knowledge of the subject as he delivers his "to camera" insights into all aspects of wine.

✔ CHECKLIST **ENSURING YOUR SITE FOLLOWS LEGAL REQUIREMENTS**

	YES	NO
• Do you list terms and conditions outlining the provisions for using your website?	☐	☐
• Do you have a privacy statement making clear your commitment to keeping users' data private?	☐	☐
• Have you used a disclaimer covering any legal responsibility for how content on your site might be used or interpreted by visitors?	☐	☐
• Do you have a copyright statement making clear that no other party has the right to reproduce the content without your permission?	☐	☐
• Does you have a notice explaining the use of cookies (if employed)?	☐	☐

Enhancing the content through images

Studies of how users read web pages suggest that hero shot* images are often ignored in favor of surrounding text and so don't achieve the same aesthetic purpose as they might in print media. Therefore, on-line, images can be a waste of space and bandwidth. However, website development is all about satisfying the needs of its visitors, and there are times when a website must include pictures, especially when they are required to describe a product in the context in which it is designed to be used. This being the case, the images should be professionally produced, with digital technology applied to present them in best fashion. While a basic picture may suffice, in some circumstances click-on enlargement may be useful to allow users to focus on some aspect of the product, or 3D technology can be used to allow the customer to move around the product to see how it looks from different angles. For example, a view from a hotel balcony can be captured so that the full vista can be seen across the webpage by the customer.

*Hero shot — *the picture on a newspaper or magazine page that appeals to the visual sense of the reader but serves no purpose in enhancing the story.*

Audio-visual formats

Audio and video are the two other formats available to the website developer. You can use them in your website to make the content richer and engage the user. The advent of the MP3 player has facilitated audio content being downloaded from a website and then listened to at the user's convenience. While this can be simply a spoken version of the site's content, it can also be recordings of interviews and seminars as well as instructions—for example, a cake recipe. Video can be a visual version of the audio options as well as being used to present a product or service—for example, a movie taken by someone moving through a house on a real estate website. As with images, audio and video content should be professionally produced to add credibility to your website.

Using widgets

Unique to digital media, widgets facilitate the delivery of live content to a website. Effective examples include tools like calculators (on a financial site), weather forecasts (for a vacation resort), or perhaps a clock showing the local time of the organization so that global users would know when an operator can take a phone call. Easy to insert, and freely available from third party providers, these pieces of scripting code can provide website developers with a variety of applications that will enhance the experience for visitors.

Effective ways to use video

INTRODUCTION
Incorporate an introduction from the owner of your organization—this can give a sense of personality.

TESTIMONIALS
Include testimonials from "real" people. Their comments will appear more valid than marketing copy.

PRODUCT DEMONSTRATIONS
Having a person show how something is done clarifies complex methods far more effectively than text alone, and also addresses safety issues.

SERVICE DEMONSTRATIONS
A demonstration enhances the visual experience of a user—for example, a guided tour of a cruise ship.

INSTRUCTIONS
Giving instructions for fitting, assembly, or maintenance becomes easier through video footage.

Creating e-commerce sites

An e-commerce site is a website that facilitates on-line transactions, taking payments through credit card or third party billing services (such as PayPal). Sometimes referred to as an e-tail site, there are aspects of such an enterprise that need careful consideration.

On-line merchandising

In an off-line environment customers can see, smell, feel, or even try out products before they make a purchase. On-line, the decision must be made on the basis of images and descriptions on screen. Think of the text as an on-line salesperson. Starting with a brief portrayal for those with existing product knowledge, descriptions should address every issue that the potential customer might question before committing to a purchase.

 PRODUCTS **DETAILS**

TIP

UP-SELL AND CROSS-SELL

Use the checkout to remind customers of upgrades, accessories, or related products that they might buy.

Checking out the checkout

If the checkout process doesn't work flawlessly then the resources spent in getting the customer to that point are wasted. The process starts when the customer puts a product in their cart. Make sure they can see their cart throughout their time shopping, and make options such as size or color easy to adjust. Also, ensure the cart "total" includes any taxes or shipping costs. Finally, make carts saveable, so customers can come back later and pick up where they left off.

Getting fulfillment right

Although delivering fulfillment is not in itself an element of the digital revolution, if you do not have the right approach all the digital elements that lead up to it are wasted. Also commonly referred to as "logistics," fulfillment is all about getting the right product to the right place at a time convenient to the recipient. It is made up of four key elements:

• **Stock control** makes sure the goods are available in an acceptable timeframe.
• **Shipping costs** must cover packaging and transport charges, and be acceptable to the customer.
• **Outbound logistics** cover the actual delivery to the customer.
• **Returns** addresses faulty or unwanted goods. These are not only strategic decisions for the organization, they have also been identified as essential in customer retention.

🛒 BUY		🚚 SHIPPING	
TO BE SHIPPED	SHIPPED	TRACKING	RECEIPTS

❓ ASK YOURSELF... DO YOU SATISFY THE FOUR TYPES OF ON-LINE BUYERS?

• Do you cater to users who are just there for some hedonistic browsing?
• Are you prepared for the buyer who is ready to purchase?
• Does your site satisfy the buyer who is researching a product, price, availability, and the terms, conditions, and credibility of the site?
• Is your site appealing enough for the explorer–browser to come back and make a purchase in the future?

Considering globalization

When you expand your organization into new countries, you must decide whether to standardize—use the same marketing mix, or localize—adapt the mix to suit the various local markets. As a digital marketer you will be faced with the same issue with regard to your global website.

Catering to a universal audience

Some domestic organizations cater to a global audience using a single website. This is usually written in the organization's home language. An English translation might be offered, or translations of some or all pages into other languages may be included. There is, however, no attempt to change the content to better suit local markets or trading environments.

EMPLOY CORRECT LANGUAGE VERSIONS
Communicate in the language version that your target market expects; US or UK English, for example.

Achieving a global website

There are organizations that develop different websites for global users, often using the suffixes of the local countries in the domain name of the website address. The content of these sites would essentially be translations of the "home" site, though the presentation and content might be adapted slightly to address local issues.

A truly global organization has its own modified website in each country, or region, in which it has a presence. The website keeps its standardized corporate design and structure but the content and presentation of these sites is adapted to address local culture and issues.

CHECK TRANSLATIONS
Have the translations checked by a native speaker. Often literal translations change the sense of the text.

Fine-tuning websites for global audiences

BE AWARE OF LOCAL CULTURE
Understand local cultures, for example, the significance of colors is different around the world.

PAY ATTENTION TO THE LINKS
Make sure the links leading to translated sites are appropriate—"Français" not "French" for a French version.

USE LOCAL METHODS
Ensure that country-specific practices are taken into account, such as correct units of measurement.

CONSIDER META-DATA
Translating invisible meta-data such as HTML tags, as search engines can pick it up; for example, Google searches in over 100 languages.

Analyzing digital footprints

The problem with marketing, particularly branding, is that it is difficult to determine the ROI. However, the digital revolution has helped marketers to address this issue. Because website visitors leave a digital footprint as they traverse the web, web analytics can tell you not only what is happening, but help to determine why it is happening.

TIP

MEASURE CORRECTLY

The number of visitors is the best measure of a site's popularity. Because a hit is a request for a single file, and a web page could be made up of dozens of files, referring to your website having a given number of hits is meaningless.

Understanding the options

Given unlimited time and resources, there is virtually no limit to the on-line statistics that can be gathered. This ranges from basic visitor counters to "experience management" software that tracks every action a visitor makes on a website, then allows you to replay a page-by-page, browser-level recording of your customer's on-site experience. While the latter is indispensable to the serious on-line trader, basic statistics such as visitor numbers, where they come from geographically, which site they were on before yours, which page they arrived on, how many pages they looked at, and how long they were on your site will probably be enough for most organizations.

Gathering data

As with much of the digital environment, the ready availability of software, most of it free, can help you gather raw data essential for your business. Most website-hosting companies provide analytics as part of the service package. Google also facilitates access to e-metrics that are adequate for the majority of website publishers. It should be noted that high-end data collection and analysis is best left to specialists in the practice, outsourcing being the best option for all but the leading e-commerce sites.

Knowing what data to measure

The ability to gather an almost infinite amount of data does not mean that all data is useful. In fact, it is only worth spending resources to gather data that can be analyzed, and which will produce useful information, ie information on the basis of which you can make decisions. Essentially, data collection should focus on the key performance indicators (KPIs) that will help assess the success—or otherwise—of the site's primary objectives. For example, an e-commerce site will, ultimately, be judged on its total sales. However, if visitor numbers are high but few make purchases, then those statistics can help the digital marketer to identify where problems might lie.

UNDERSTANDING WEBSITE ANALYTICS

WEBSITE'S OBJECTIVE	VISITOR NUMBERS	NUMBER OF REPEAT VISITS	HOW DEEP VISITORS GO	ACTIONS COMPLETED
Brand development	High numbers represent more brand exposure.	Repeated visits show brand loyalty.	Searching deeper means more brand involvement.	Not important as direct action is not the site's main purpose.
Customer service and support	A high number is good as off-line resources are relieved, but it could also indicate problems with the product.	A high number might signify that visitors have not been satisfied on earlier visits.	Going deep can mean that visitors are seeking a solution but can also mean that information is hard to find.	A low number is bad, as it indicates visitors have not found what they were looking for.
Income generation	A high number is good only if it translates into a high number of purchase actions.	A high number of repeat visits suggest brand loyalty.	Exploring deeper is good but could mean that visitors are struggling to find what they want.	It is bad if actions are not being completed as this is the main purpose of the website.

Digital market intelligence

Although website analytics can provide a wealth of research data on customer activities in relation to your web presence, the digital environment provides the organization with wider access to useful information that was previously only available to off-line researchers.

BEWARE OF THE RESTRICTED SAMPLE
An inherent problem in conducting surveys on-line is that the only respondents are those who have access to the web—making the sample potentially flawed.

Gathering primary data

All methods of collecting primary data using the Internet are on-line applications of traditional off-line techniques—but they can be more effective, and certainly cheaper. The Internet makes distribution of survey questionnaires very easy, and the interactive nature of the web can increase response rates. These can range from single questions posed in a small box in a prominent position on a busy site, to full-blown questionnaires accessed from a link—a banner or a pop-up promoting the survey—or by e-mail.

Sourcing secondary information

Traditionally available in libraries and by mail order, detailed market data is now available on-line from research organizations such as Mintel and Keynote. Trade associations and local Chambers of Commerce also frequently publish industry and market data that is freely available on their websites. Governments make a point of publishing data on-line, and on a multi-national scale, the World Trade Organization uses its website (wto.org) to publish global trade statistics. For on-going environmental and industry information, news sites, blogs, and press releases are available by visiting websites or signing up for e-newsletters. Social media sites, in particular those with user generated content, can also be a source of constructive market information.

Digital Spying

It has always been common practice for businesses to track competitors' activities, and simply gathering information in the public domain—on- and off-line—is an expected aspect of doing business. Using the 4Ps as a guide, you can look for products offered by competitors, how much they are charging, how they are distributing their products, and what promotions and activities they are participating in.

READ THE LATEST NEWS
Stay abreast of news and happenings in the industry in general and in your market.

CHECK REVIEWS
Read what customers have to say about you and your competitors on "review sites" and in blogs.

LOOK FOR WAYS TO EXPAND
Find new markets by, perhaps, visiting the websites of organizations that might use your products.

SCAN FOR NEW IDEAS
Develop new products by tracking the websites of industry leaders, to "adopt" their ideas.

Chapter 4

Promoting through digital media

The digital revolution has provided organizations with a new medium to reach customers with promotional messages. Taking advantage of this new medium requires some new skills to ensure your messages are effective.

Optimizing your website

Mastering search engine optimization (SEO) is essential to succeed in the digital marketplace. The influence of search engines on the digital environment is such that in many respects digital marketing is effectively search-engine marketing.

Appreciating SEO

*SERP —
Search Engine Results, or Returns, Page. It is the web page on which search results are presented to the searcher.

SEO is the practice of making a website attractive to a search engine, by presenting information in such a way that the search engine will calculate that this site addresses a specific inquiry from a human searcher. Contrary to popular opinion, the aim of SEO is not to get the better of the search engines. Search engines want to satisfy their users by listing sites whose content matches the searchers' requirements, and by doing so generate revenue from advertising on their SERPs*. Search engines therefore need websites as much as website publishers need search engines.

Understanding how SEO works

Search engines work by trawling ("spidering")
the web to collect details of as many websites as
possible. When a user performs a search, the search
engine assesses websites in its index for relevance
to the search criteria using its own algorithm. The
algorithm is the core of SEO, and its formula is kept
secret by the search engine. At the crux of all SEO
are keywords, the words or phrases that the searcher
types into the search box. It is essential that the
digital marketer matches the keywords for which their
website is optimized with those used by the searcher.
For example, you might market "best value"
products, but consumers search for "cheap" ones.
Searchers may also use their reason for a purchase
as keywords—if you sell toys, "children's birthday
presents" might be a suitable phrase for which to
optimize a web page.

Experts agree that SEO centers around two distinct
categories: (1) elements concerned with the website
itself (on-site), and (2) elements outside the
parameters of the site (off-site).

ASK YOURSELF... HOW IMPORTANT IS SEARCH ENGINE OPTIMIZATION TO YOU?

- Is your business dependent on on-line sales?
- Is your ratio of on-line sales higher than off-line?
- Is the primary objective of your site income generation?
- Can customers find your website without using search engines?
- Does your off-line marketing bring more customers to your website?
- How competitive is your market? How are you and your competitors placed
  in the SERPs?
- Do you sell a niche product that buyers will spend time seeking?
- If you operate in a B2B industry, how important is the web in procurement
  decision making?

On-site optimization

On-site optimization means placing keywords in the right places on the web page. Keywords should crop up naturally in the content; for example, a page about diamonds would include words like clarity and carat in the text. However, the text can be tweaked to improve SEO. Search engines try to read a page as a human would, for example giving higher priority to header text. They also try to assess the credibility of sites. An on-line diamond store with no physical address or terms and conditions section, for example, would be ranked lower than a site (with the same keywords) that did. Keywords can also be placed in the site's source code, including in the page's title tag, alt attributes for images, and H1 tags (instructions for page or paragraph headers).

TOOLS
Offer functional help to the user, for example, an on-line directory of industry terms will attract other related sites to link to yours.

Ways to attract links to your site

CONTRARY OPINIONS
Take up a contrary stance to an expert or public opinion on a given subject related to your industry—these might take the form of an article

NEWS
Feature news items on your site offering specific and credible information about the market or industry that other sites will link to.

LISTS
Publish "lists" on your website—these are very popular with consultants looking to sell their services, for example, "Five ways to attract links."

RESOURCES
Make your website a source of industry information. Articles or research results, for example, can be posted on your website to make it informative.

Off-site optimization

Off-site elements now carry increasing weight in SEO. Although the website's history and credibility are considered (how long it has existed, for example, or how frequently it is updated), search engines also give preference to sites linked to by other sites, as it is assumed that they carry some legitimacy with the linking sites. It is not just the quantity of these links that counts. Search engines also give greater authority to links from academic sites with domains like .edu and .ac.uk. The relevance of the linking site is also important. A link from a soccer page to one on gardening, for example would carry no validity.

Advertising on-line

Placing advertisements in traditional media such as newspapers, TV, and magazines, is an effective practice that dates back centuries. However, after years of being dismissed as a poor alternative to the established media, increasing amounts of advertising dollars are now moving on-line, a reflection that the digital age has truly arrived.

Setting objectives

Like traditional advertising, on-line advertising has three main objectives:
• **Direct action**—seeking to elicit a reaction from consumers
• **Lead generation**—common in B2B, looking to start off a procurement dialog
• **Branding**—for a brand, organization, or product.

Having set objectives, you will need to decide whether to out-source your advertising or have it done in-house. Contracting out will normally ensure that the right advertisements appear in the most appropriate media at the right time, but at a cost.

Deciding where to place your advertisement is also important. On-line networks have made it easy for even the smallest website to host advertisements, increasing the options for advertisers. Your advertisement can be matched with the content of the website to make it more relevant.

Choosing the format

Essentially, there are two formats available on-line—textual and banner advertisements. The choice of format is largely determined by the objectives for the advertisement and where they are to be displayed. Although objectives are controlled by the advertiser, it is the nature of the publishing site that will determine the presentation of the advertisement. Text advertisements, which appear in SERP and network advertising, are generally regarded as best for direct action, while banners, which appear across the top, bottom, or down the side of web pages, are better for overall branding.

Pop-up advertisements have a bad reputation, and their use has been reduced by blocking software. However, it is worth noting that they remain statistically the most successful kind of banner advertisement, and can be very effective if used judiciously.

Paying for on-line advertising

COST PER THOUSAND IMPRESSIONS (CPM) – used for banner advertisements; payment relates to how often the ad is shown.

PAY PER CLICK (PPC)— the advertiser pays the host website only when their advertisement is clicked on by a user.

PAY PER CALL – the host website receives a fee every time a call is made to a featured phone number.

COMPARING TRADITIONAL WITH ON-LINE ADVERTISING

	TRADITIONAL ADVERTISING	ON-LINE ADVERTISING
Advantages	• Agencies and advertisers are familiar with the medium and easy to find • Skills, tools, and techniques are well developed and practised • Rates are well-established	• On-line advertising is interactive • Potential for instant results • Advertising content can be matched to the content of the website to increase relevance • Digital technology facilitates analysis • PPC means paying only for successful ads • Web pages must be requested by the user, creating an element of self-segmentation
Disadvantages	• Pushes out the message with little targeting • ROI difficult to assess • Fixed broadcast times • Communication is one-way	• New skills and methods required • Wariness of new technology and a lack of understanding of how digital works • No peak viewing hours—individuals browse at their own pace

THINK LOCAL

As local advertising gains prominence, you can use sites like Google Maps, Microsoft Live Search, and Yahoo! Local to reach regional customers.

Targeting your advertisements

Although the concept of target marketing is as old as advertising itself, delivering your advertisements only to your target market is easier in the digital age. While traditional advertising is limited to broad segmentation, on-line advertising includes an element of self-segmentation by the user. The Internet is a pull medium—the user must request a web page—and as search engine and network advertisements are keyword generated, the advertisements delivered on these pages are matched to the content. So if a site offers advice on driving, the advertisements on that page might be for car insurance. And if it offers advice for young drivers, the advertisements could be for insurance for under-21s and so on.

On-line advertisement delivery has two key types of targeting:

• **Contextual** where the ads served are relevant to the content of the web page.

• **Behavioral** where ads are delivered in response to prior on-line activities of a customer.

A third, which can be used in conjunction with the first two, is geographical, where IP recognition is used to identify in which part of the world the surfer is located advertisements are selected accordingly.

✓ CHECKLIST GETTING NETWORK ADVERTISING RIGHT

	YES	NO
• Have I selected the right keywords?	☐	☐
• Have I determined the ROI on PPC costs for those keywords?	☐	☐
• Have I written enticing copy with distinct offers—and included a call-to-action?	☐	☐
• Have I developed landing pages that lead respondents to an action that fulfills the objectives of the advertisement?	☐	☐

Designing landing pages

An essential part of the sales funnel, landing pages are those pages to which a respondent is taken when they click on an on-line advertisement—and they should be designed with as much attention as the advertisements themselves. Think of them as an extension of the advertisement—if an advertisement motivates a potential customer to click on it, the sales momentum must be sustained, hopefully all the way through to the "buy now" command. Each landing page must be designed for the advertisement that links to it—simply sending potential customers to your site's homepage is a serious error. Of particular value is the ability of the landing page to segment visitors by which stage of the buying process they are on. Someone clicking on a hotel advertisement, for example, might be looking to make a reservation or just weighing up alternatives. An effective landing page should be able to forward each visitor to the relevant part of the hotel's website.

Advertising on mobile devices

Long touted as the "next big thing," advertising on mobile devices is finally showing signs of coming into its own. Although what constitutes a "mobile device" is debatable (a laptop can be mobile), with regard to digital advertising the term refers to handheld equipment that can connect to the web, such as cell phones and personal digital assistants (PDAs). Although there are technical issues with formatting content for small screens, mobile can be an effective medium for advertisers. Services such as travel or theater tickets, for example, can be popular among last-minute purchasers. And the devices' global positioning systems (GPS) can be used to serve advertisements that are relevant geographically—perhaps for a café close to the user's current location.

Advertising through keywords

Advertising on search engines is not the same as being featured in organic SERP listings. Instead, organizations bid to place text advertisements alongside organic listings when a search is made for a given keyword or phrase. Network advertising uses similar principles.

Understanding the concept

**Bounce rate —
the percentage of
people who after
landing on a page
immediately return
to the site they came
from. A high bounce
rate generally
indicates that the
landing pages
aren't relevant to
the visitors.*

Search-engine advertising often appears alongside normal search results on the SERP (search engine results page). However, in search engine advertising, instead of pages being selected on the basis of relevance to the search, the keywords are bought by the advertiser through a bidding system. The advertisement highest on the SERP's sponsored listings will be the one with the best bid. The best bid is not always the highest bid; other influencing factors include:

• **Clickthrough rate (CTR)** Advertisers whose advertisements attract a lot of clicks gain extra credit.

• **Quality of landing pages** This is based on factors such as bounce rate*, keyword relevance in headings and body copy, and the site's business model.

🔍 IN FOCUS... CLICK FRAUD

Click fraud refers to the event of a clickthrough that is not made by a genuine customer. Mistakes do take place, but businesses are worried by multiple clickthroughs that are deliberate attempts to defraud the advertiser. Because the advertiser pays the publisher of the website on which it appears a fee every time a user clicks on that advertisement, it is the publisher who benefits from nefarious clicks. The dishonest publisher pays accomplices to make repeated clicks—obviously paying them less per click than the advertiser will pay for those clickthroughs.

Having won the bidding at a set price, that fee is payable to the search engine every time a potential customer clicks on your advertisement. This concept is also known as pay per click (PPC). A key advantage of buying advertisements is that it gives the digital marketer a degree of control over the situation, whereas SEO results are far from certain.

In network advertising, the advertisements are published on pages whose publisher has opted to feature network advertisements (for a percentage of the PPC fee). Rather than matching search keywords, these advertisements match purchased keywords with the textual content of the web page.

Bidding for keywords

Keyword bidding is influenced by the level of competition, so some keywords cost more than others. Effective search and network advertising is based on getting the highest number of conversions at a cost that will facilitate a realistic profit. This means weighing higher cost but better conversions—visits from a customer that result in a purchase—against lower cost advertisements that don't result in many conversions. Considerations in effective keyword bidding include:

• **Keyword matching options** Choose from general, exact, negative words, or a phrase.

• **Cost of keywords** Consider the popular, but expensive keywords, against those that are rarely used and inexpensive.

• **Differentiators** Use adjectives that describe keywords more specifically.

• **Branded keywords** These can be effective but may infringe trademark legislation.

• **Scheduling** Have advertisements appear only when your target audience is on-line.

• **Demographic targeting** Target users by gender or age, but expect the options for targeting to expand.

HOW TO... ADVERTISE USING "PAY PER CLICK"

Select appropriate keywords that your potential customers might use.

↓

Develop the textual content carefully so the advertisement will appeal to your target market.

↓

Make a suitable bid for the keyword(s) against your competitors in the market.

↓

Be sure you make the best bid to be placed on top of the "sponsored listings."

↓

Pay a fee to the search engine or the network only when a user clicks on your advertisement.

Exploring DOOH advertising

Driven by increasingly liberal regulation of technology, digital out-of-home (DOOH) media is growing fast, replacing its traditional "static" forerunner and reaching locations not available to advertisers previously. It is used extensively to advertise food and drink, consumer packaged goods (CPG), electronics, and entertainment.

Understanding DOOH

DOOH media is digital signage that is displayed in public spaces (airports, office buildings, hospitals and medical centers, and concert venues), social places (bars, restaurants, cafes, university campuses), and retail environments. Digital technology is used to present dynamic advertisements, particularly in environments where the viewer has time to absorb a longer message, for example, on public transport. DOOH can be all-encompassing or intimate. For example, banks of 70-inch LCD panels allow commercials to envelop the consumer, while digital display boards on restaurant tables can flash dining information such as daily specials as well as generic advertising. Significant advantages of this medium include:

• **High visibility** In some places, it can be impossible not to look at.

• **Reaching a specific audience** It has the ability to target a demographic based on the location or time of day.

• **Gesture-based technology** It can sense a passing customer's motion and trigger a suitable message.

ASK YOURSELF...
HAVE I GOT DOOH ADVERTISING RIGHT?

- Have I established my target market?
- Is the format appropriate for the target market?
- Is the content right for the medium, and for potential buyers?
- Is it in the right environment and at the right time?
- Have I established an appropriate measurement to determine ROI?

Using DOOH to your advantage

Viewers of DOOH media are typically either moving from one place to another, standing in a line, or involved in another primary activity such as shopping or eating. Therefore, to effectively get your message across you must appreciate that these different kinds of viewers need different kinds of content. Key considerations include:

• Digital signage is most effective when clear, short text messages are presented with graphics and motion.

• The text should be easily readable, state the subject and value proposition, and include an explicit "call-to-action," for example, directions to a website, location, or phone number.

• To make it more appealing, motion can be used to change the text, and graphics can zoom in or out or move around the screen or produce flashing or blinking effects.

• The duration should be in context of how long the sign will be seen—fleeting or over a longer period—although the digital nature of the medium means that message variations can be easily incorporated.

• Complex messages are rarely displayed on DOOH screens; the best digital signage present basic information and asks for action in a straightforward way.

TIP

RESEARCH THE TIMING
DOOH advertisements can be tailored not only to the time of day, but to the date, month, or season in which they're shown. Research the best times to advertise your organization and tailor your message accordingly.

CASE STUDY

Interactive digital signage
Revelers in New York City's Times Square on New Year's Eve 2008 were some of the first people to see and play with MegaPhone Inc's multiplayer cell-phone controlled game. Sponsored by the Bank of America, the game was a football trivia challenge in which viewers used their cell phones to call a number displayed on screen, and then answer questions using their keypads. Up to 500 players could join the game and compete in real time. For Megaphone it proved to be an excellent launch for their new product, and their sponsorship allowed Bank of America to reach a target audience that was otherwise largely out of their reach.

Marketing through e-mail

Despite the influx of spam that arrives in our e-mail inboxes everyday, direct marketing using e-mail still gives the best ROI of all digital marketing.

Preparing e-mails

Lists of e-mail addresses can be rented from agencies, but it is better to develop your own from customer lists, sales enquiries, or competitions and prize draws. However, it is essential that anyone you contact gives permission for you to e-mail them.

The e-mail marketer must work hard to elicit a response from the reader. The first obstacle is that only two lines of your e-mail are visible in the reader's inbox: the subject line and the sender's details. The sender may have some influence but the subject line is key. If that short message is attractive, the e-mail will be opened. As with many marketing messages, the subject line can seek to solve a problem faced by the intended receiver ("how to beat those tax-return blues") or present an urgent communication ("last chance to…"). The message itself should expand on the subject line, and include a call to action that will take the user to a landing page.

Sending a marketing e-mail is more complicated than putting a letter in the mail. Your message may be blocked by spam filters, and it may appear differently for different customers according to which e-mail service they use. Test by opening e-mail accounts with as many different providers as possible, and send a test e-mail to each address.

7
MEASURE RESPONSE
Measure how many e-mails result in a purchase.

6
SEND
Send the e-mail and consider a follow-up for time-sensitive promotions.

Developing an e-mail campaign

1
SET OBJECTIVES
Determine the key objectives and target market of the campaign.

2
COMPILE A MAILING LIST
Make or rent a list of willing customers.

3
CREATE CONTENT
Include an attractive subject line and text, with a call to action.

4
PREPARE LANDING PAGES
Ensure it offers a chance to purchase.

5
TEST
Test the technology by sending to different systems.

Communicating by e-mail

When considering e-mail in a marketing perspective it is easy to think only of its direct marketing application. Too often, organizations forget that e-mail is a medium of communication—and one that can be both an efficient and effective. E-mails to customers should be as carefully managed as any other form of content.

Writing personal response e-mails

Personal response e-mails require an individual response and come in two forms: business related (coming from suppliers, vendors, or job applicants) and those coming from customers. All incoming e-mails should be handled with equal attention. Whatever your response, add a personal touch by writing as an individual, not as a corporation. Put your name at the end of each e-mail, and add your off-line address and other contact details.

Developing outgoing e-mails

All too often, e-mails are sent without considering how their content may impact the organization's marketing efforts. All e-mail responses should adhere to a designated protocol. You can achieve this by following some simple practices:

- **Assign named respondents**, especially for sales or customer enquiries, who will take responsibility in meeting the needs of the customer.
- **Ensure prompt replies** to all incoming e-mails.
- **Use a corporate or brand appearance** by making templates for e-mail presentation.
- **Have a uniform style for the text**, including a pre-determined salutation, sign-off, and spelling conventions, as well as the tone of the message.

Improving automated e-mails

For many organizations, particularly those in e-commerce, the bulk of out-going e-mail traffic is repetitive in nature—essentially, the same message going to different people. In these cases digital technology can be used to generate automated—triggered—responses to a customer's actions or other events. As with all outgoing e-mails, the triggered e-mail has a marketing purpose to serve, and so must be crafted carefully. For example, "thanks for your order, we will be processing it and will let you know when it is despatched" is a much better response than "your order has been received." As a digital manager, realize that even automated e-mail responses help build relationships with customers, and simply "humanizing" each response is a minimum requirement.

RESPONDING TO E-MAILS

FAST TRACK	OFF TRACK
Designating employees to prioritize and respond to incoming e-mails	Letting e-mails pile up in a generic inbox until someone has time to sort and respond to them
Forwarding e-mails to someone with the expertise to respond	Letting anyone reply—whether or not it is their area of expertise
Sending a reply within one working day acknowledging the e-mail, following up with a full response	Not bothering to confirm that a response has been received
Training staff on how to write e-mails, and providing them with standard templates or drafts	Not checking with the sender that they are satisfied with the response

Index

Acknowledgments

Author's acknowledgments
Thanks to all at DK—in particular Dan Mills.

If this book whetted your appetite for the subject, there is a lot more information on the author's website:
www.alancharlesworth.eu

Publisher's acknowledgments
The publisher would like to thank Margaret Parrish and Charles Wills for coordinating Americanization.

Picture credits
The publisher would like to thank the following for their kind permission to reproduce their photographs:

1 Gettty: Nick Koudis; 4–5 Getty: Ian McKinnell; 8 iStockphoto.com: Andrey Prokhorov; 10–11 Getty: Alfred Gescheidt; 21 Getty Images: James Forte; 23 iStockphoto.com: Luis Carlos Torres;

28 Getty: Hans; 30–31 iStockphoto.com: Martin Sach; 40 Corbis: Sean Davey; 44–45 iStockphoto.com: Kiyoshi Takahase Segundo; 48–49 Getty: Glowimages; 53 (background) Corbis: Josh Westrich; 53 iStockphoto.com: Michal Mrozek; 56–57 Getty: Photodisc; 59 iStockphoto.com: bubaone; 66–67 Corbis: David Woods

Jacket images: Front: Getty Images: Chris Thomaidis

All other images © Dorling Kindersley For further information see:
www.dkimages.com